AF608726

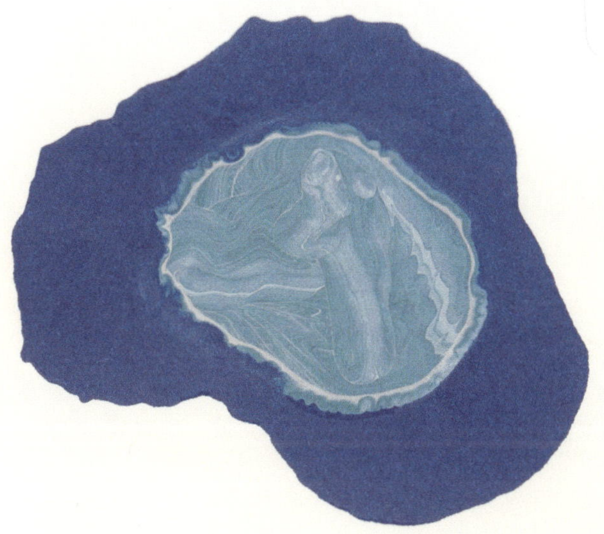

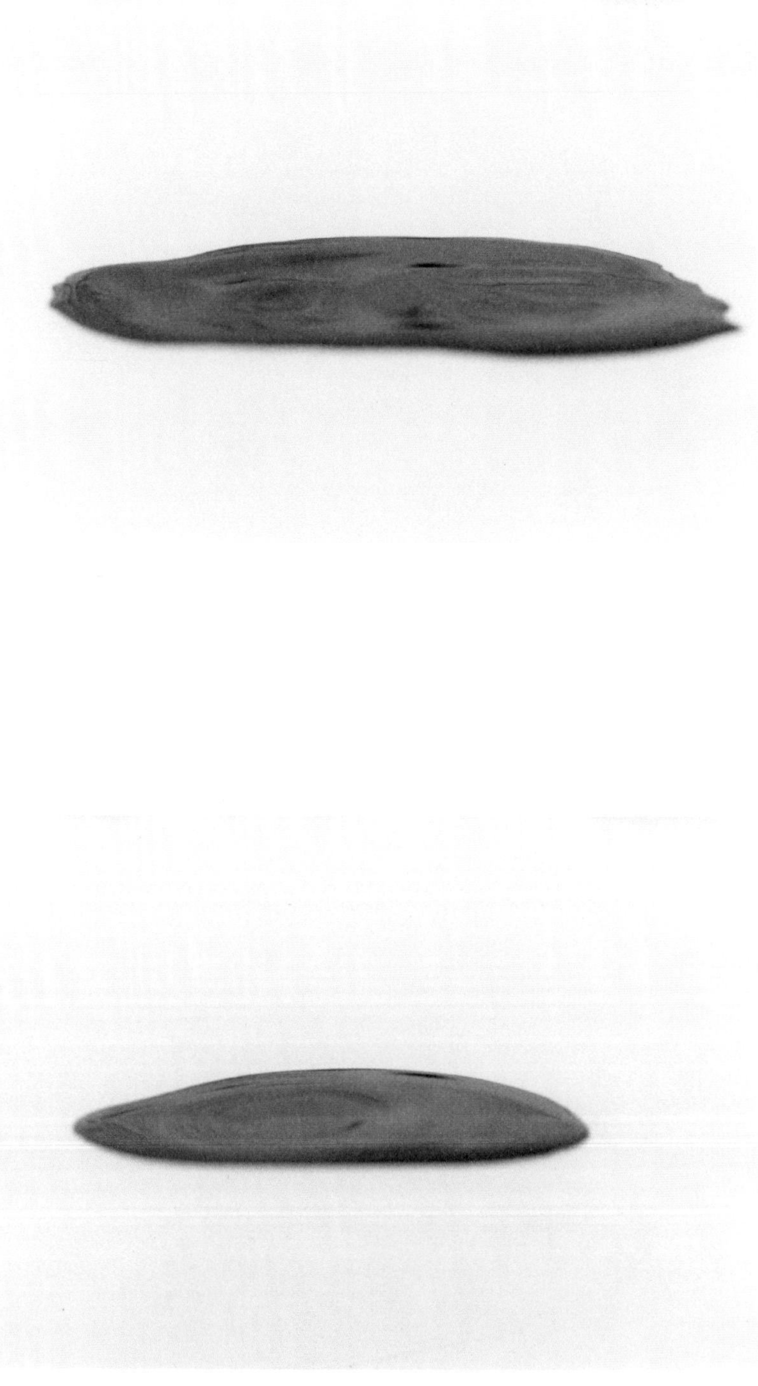

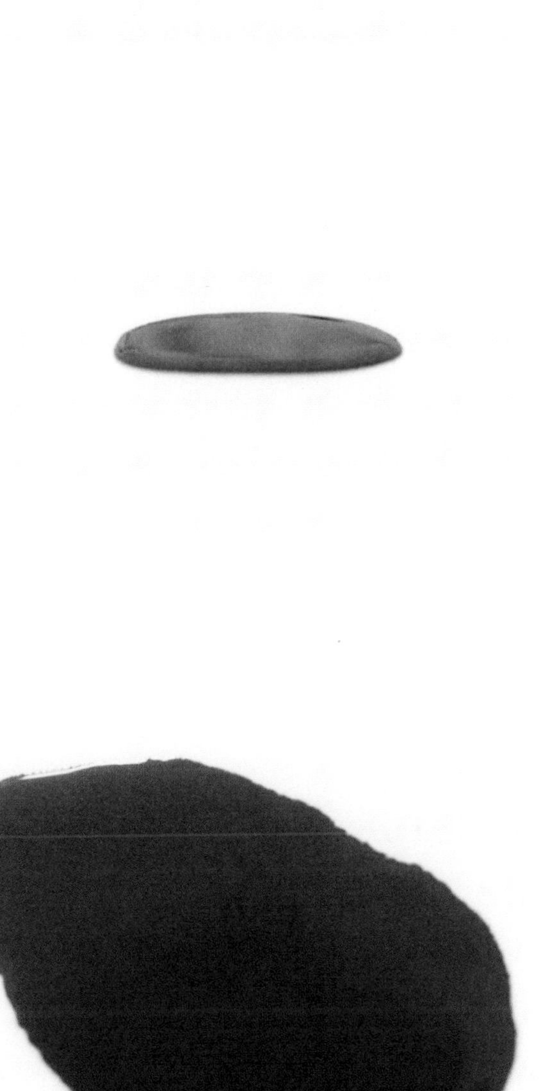

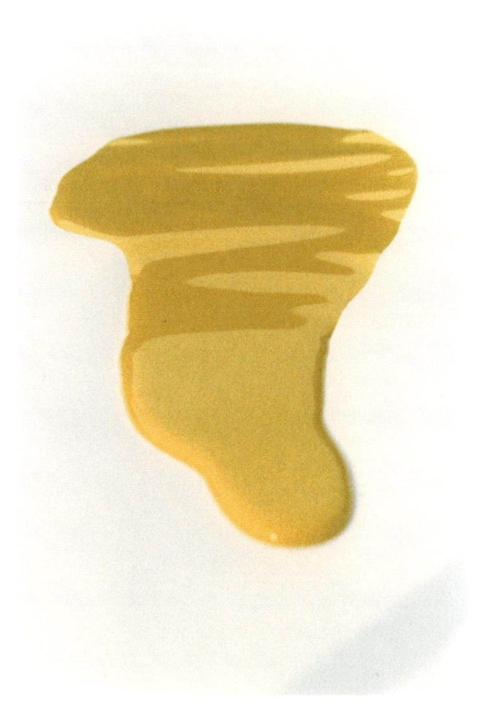

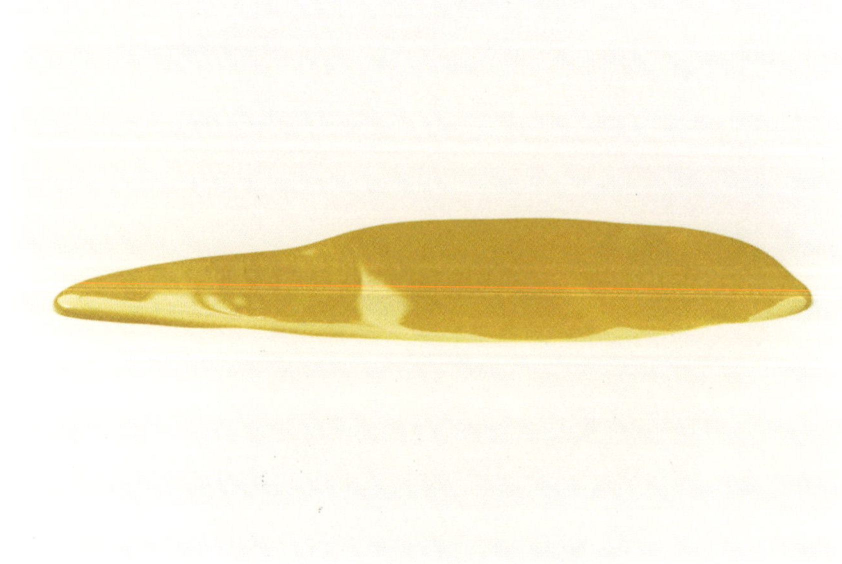

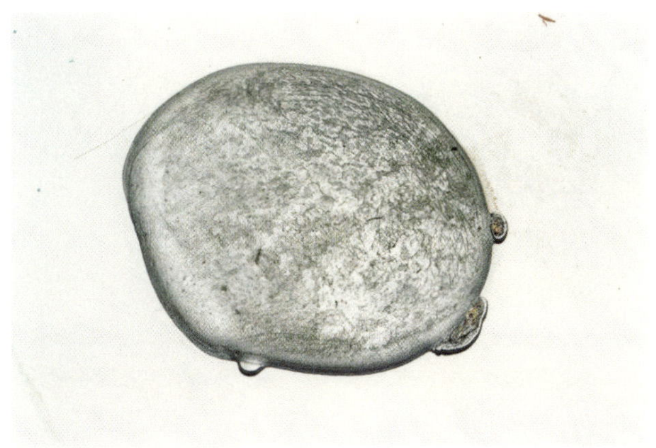

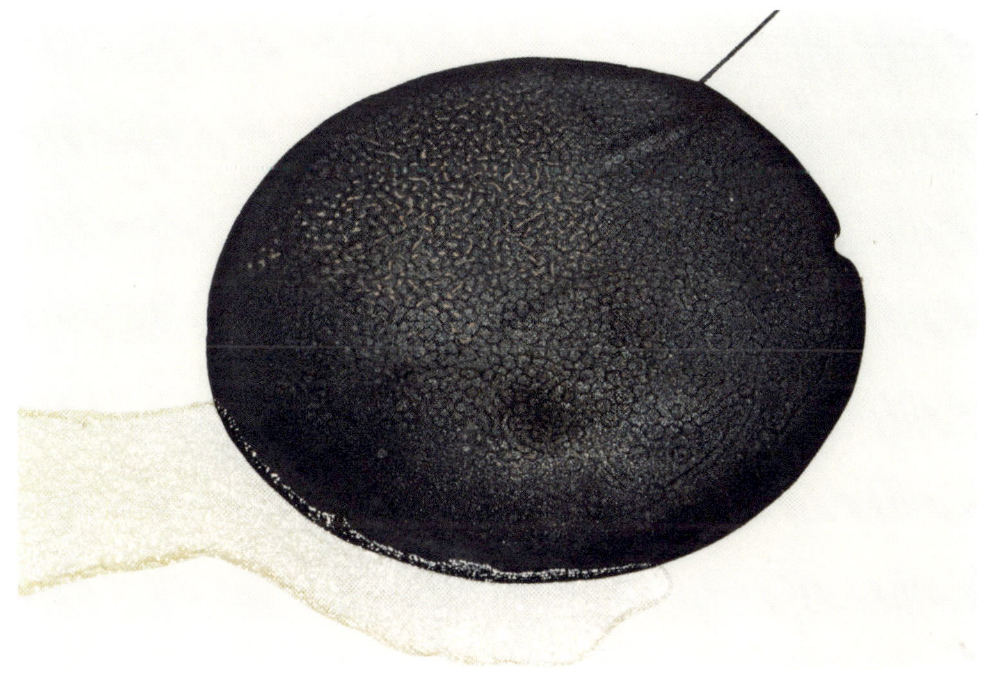

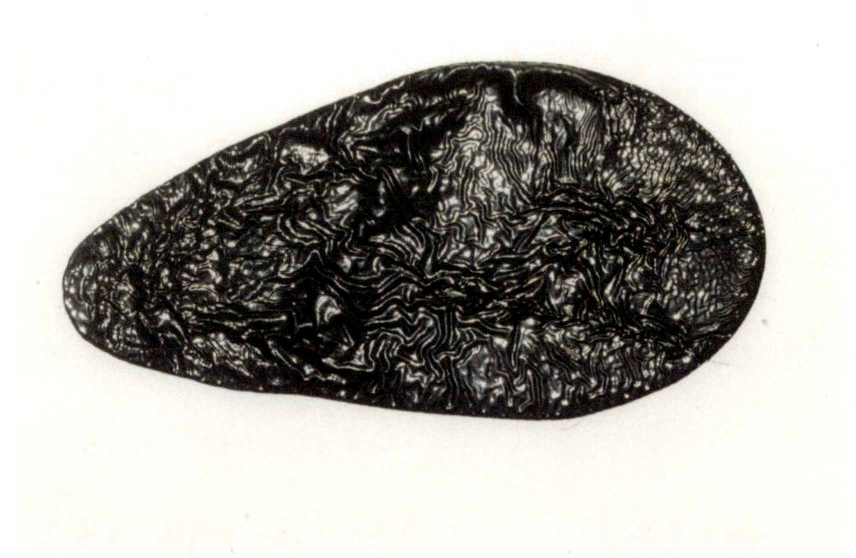

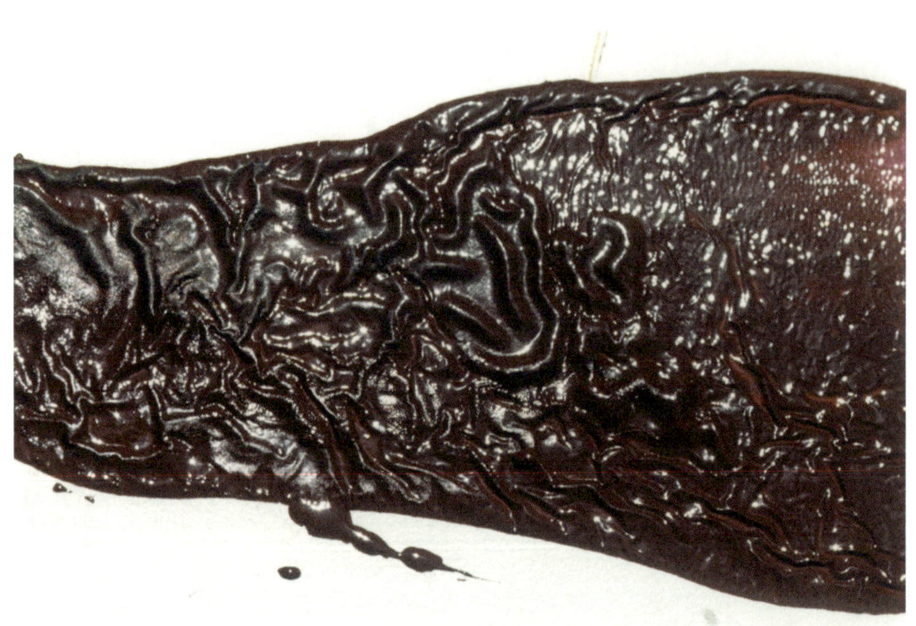

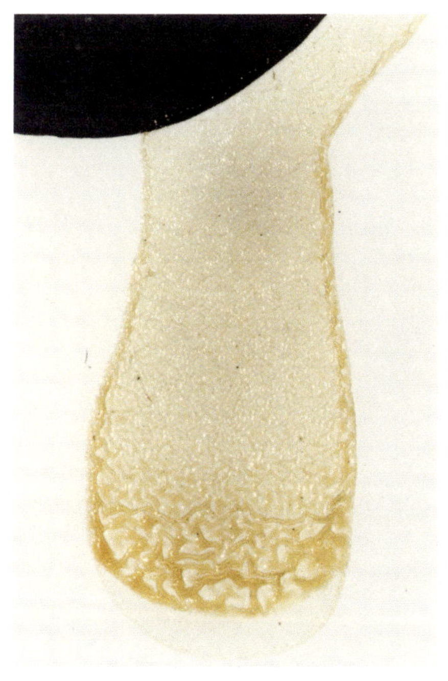

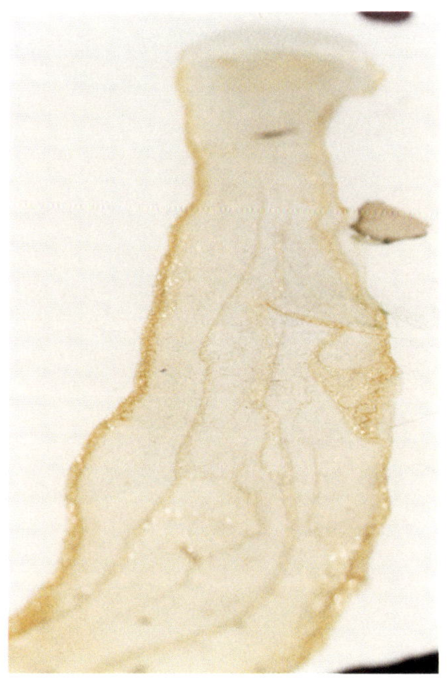

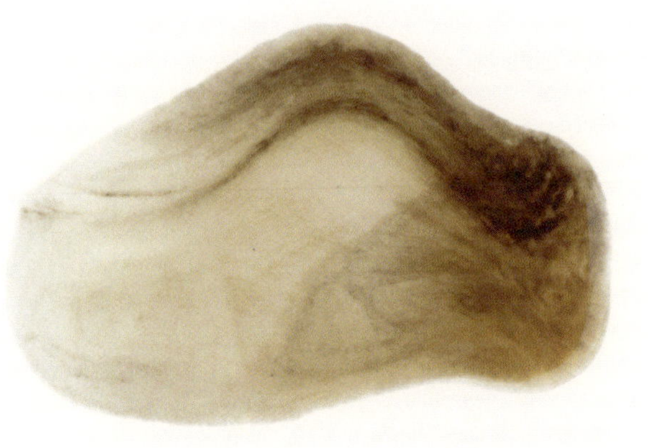

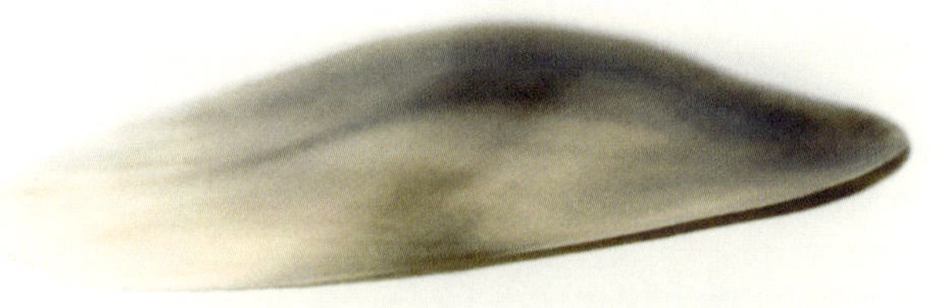

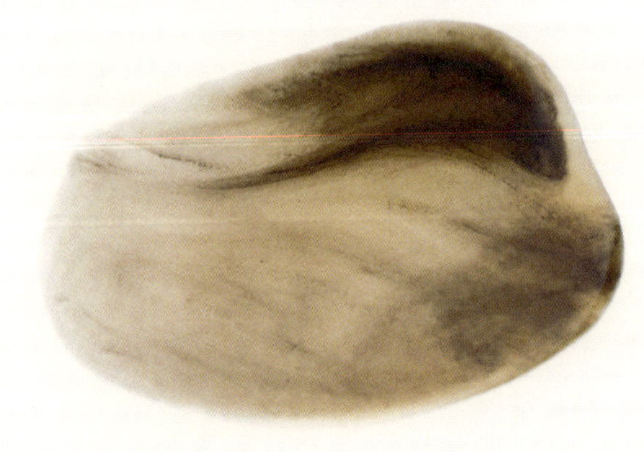

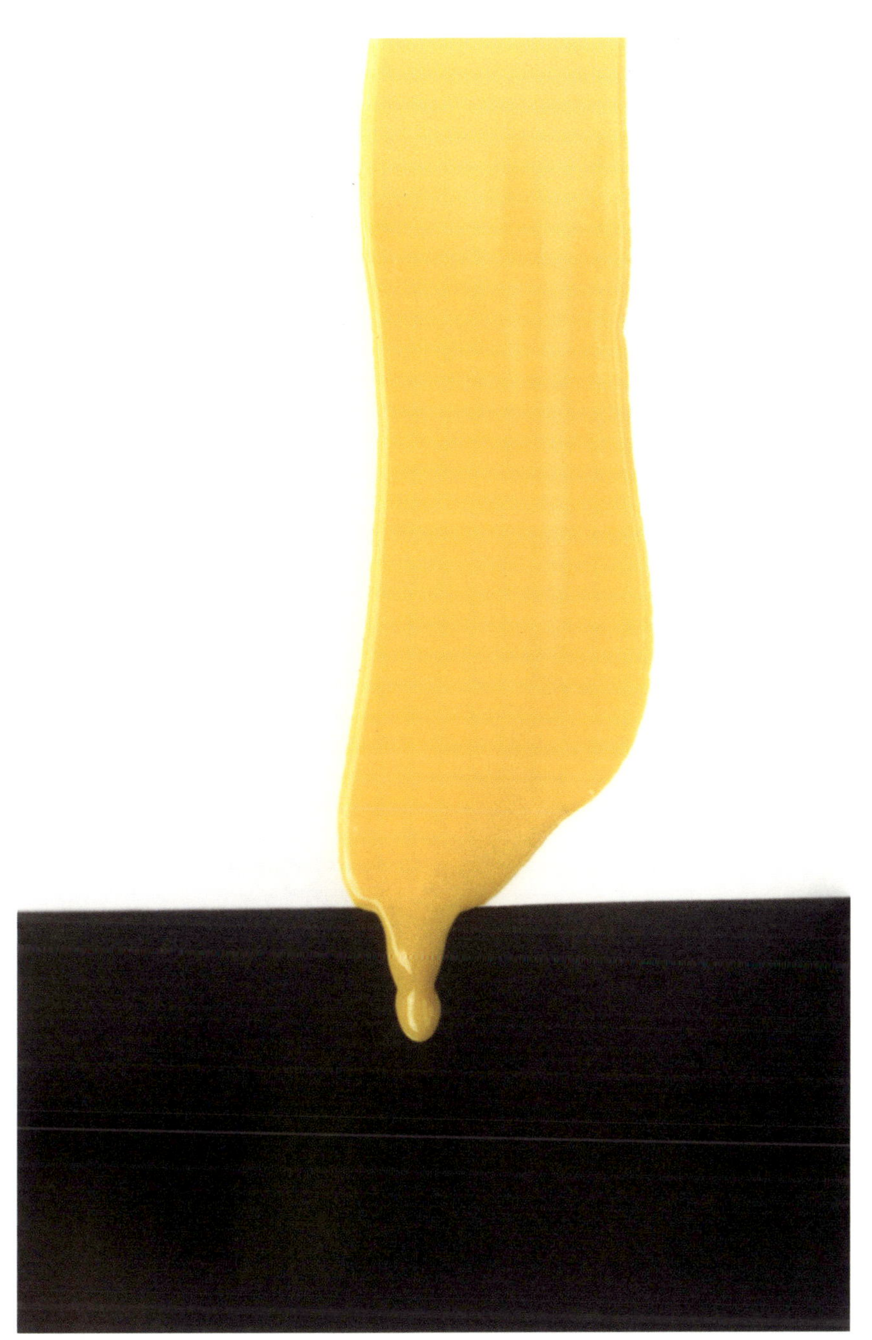

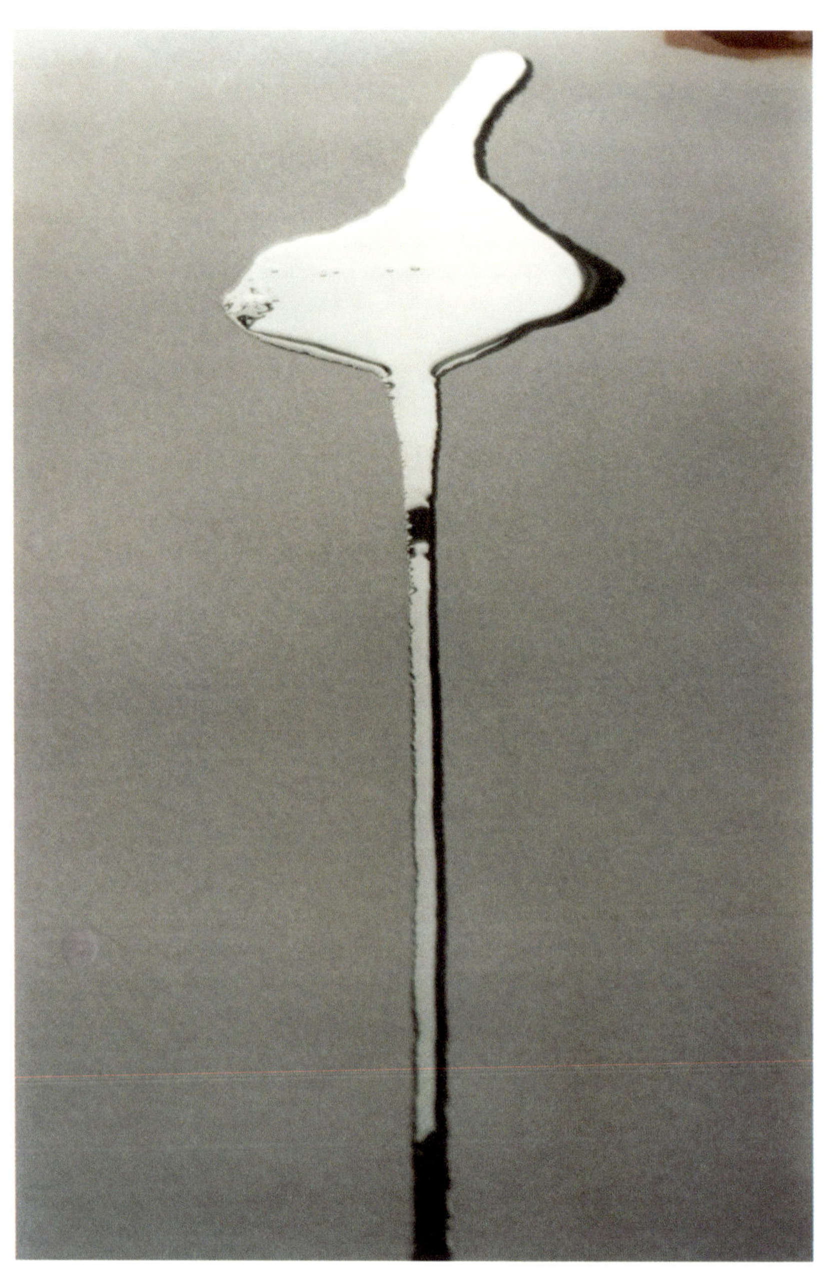

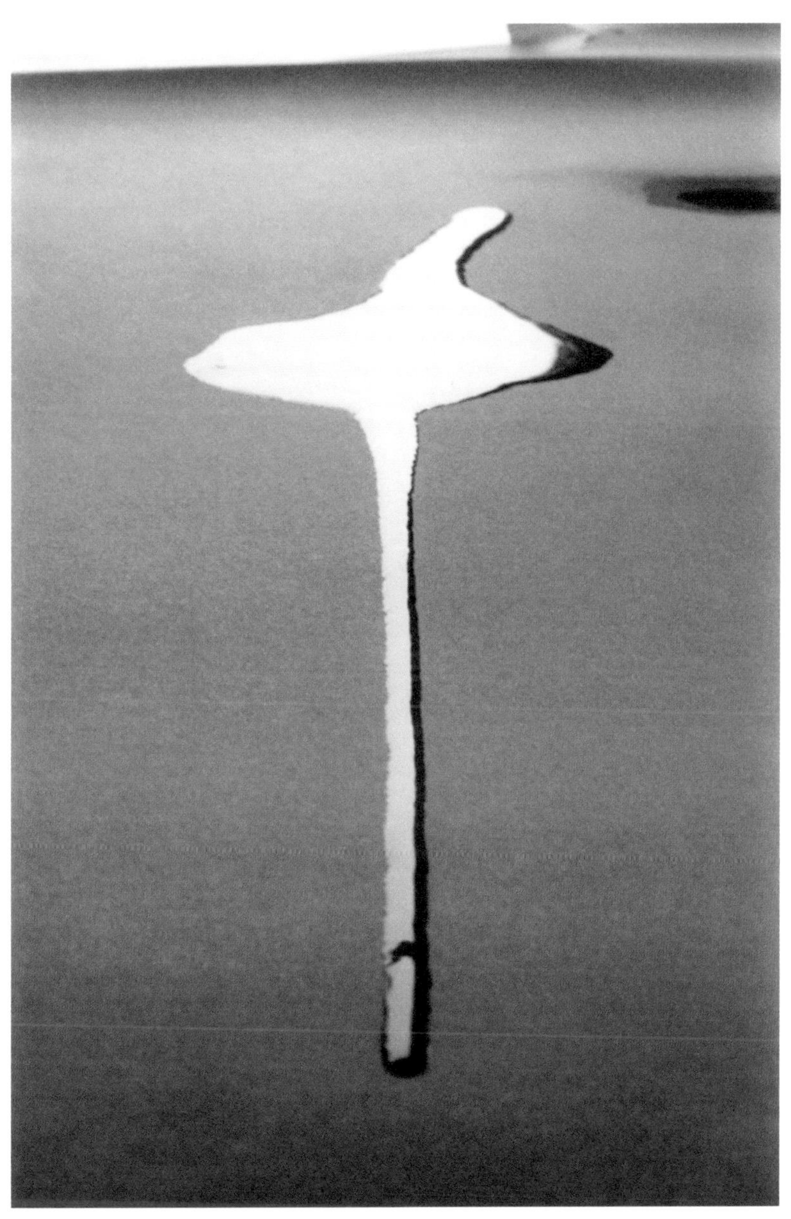

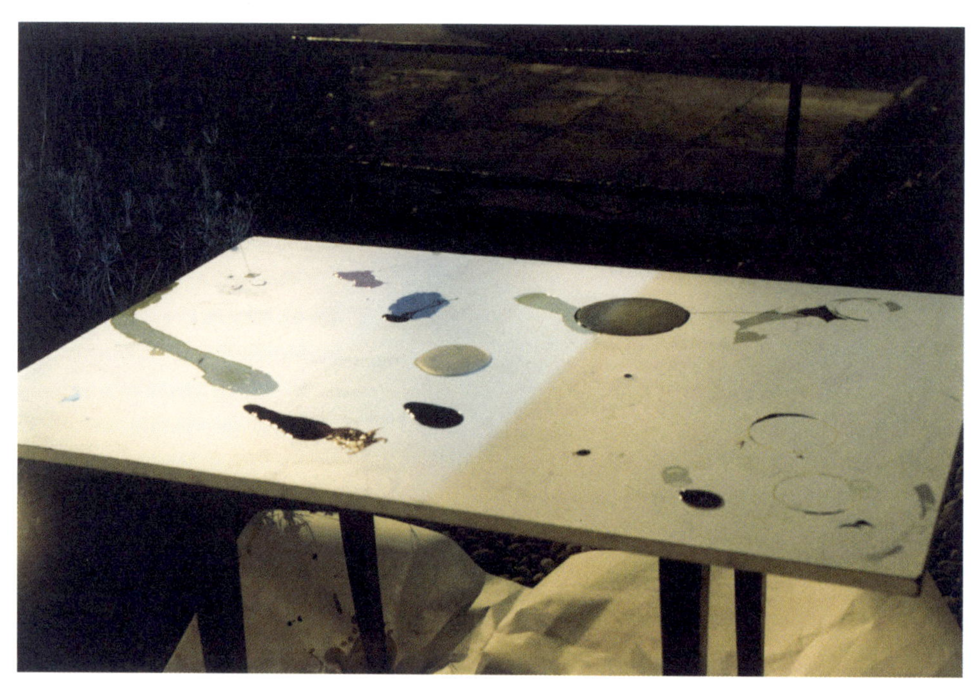

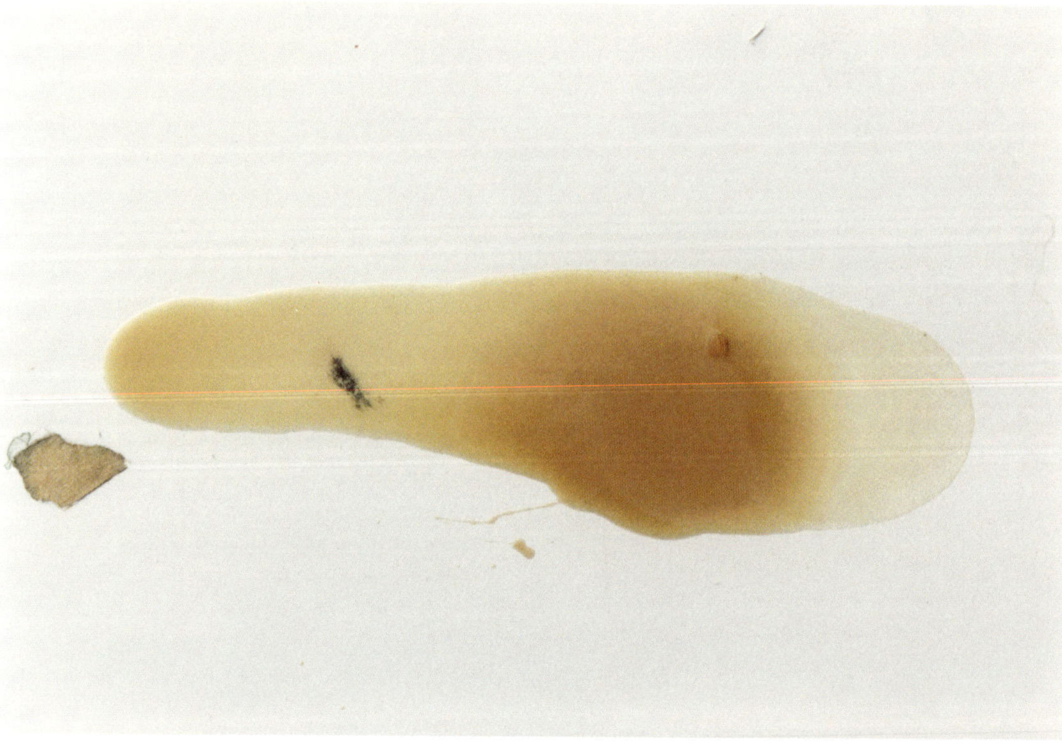

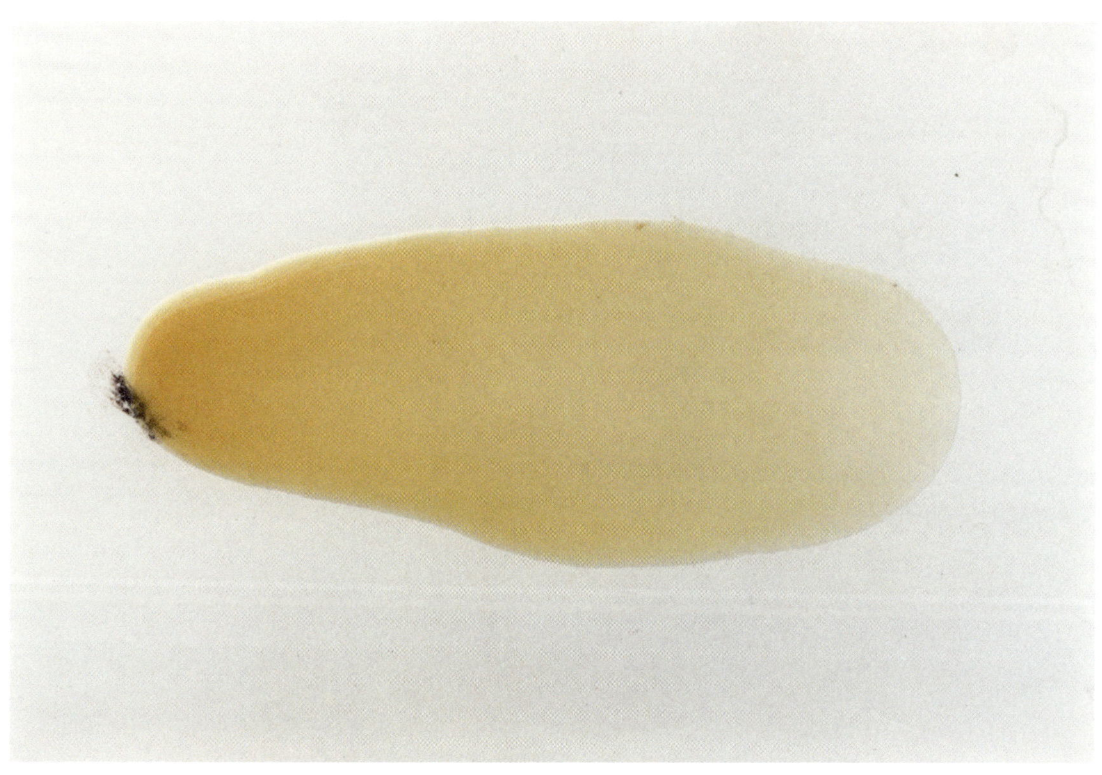

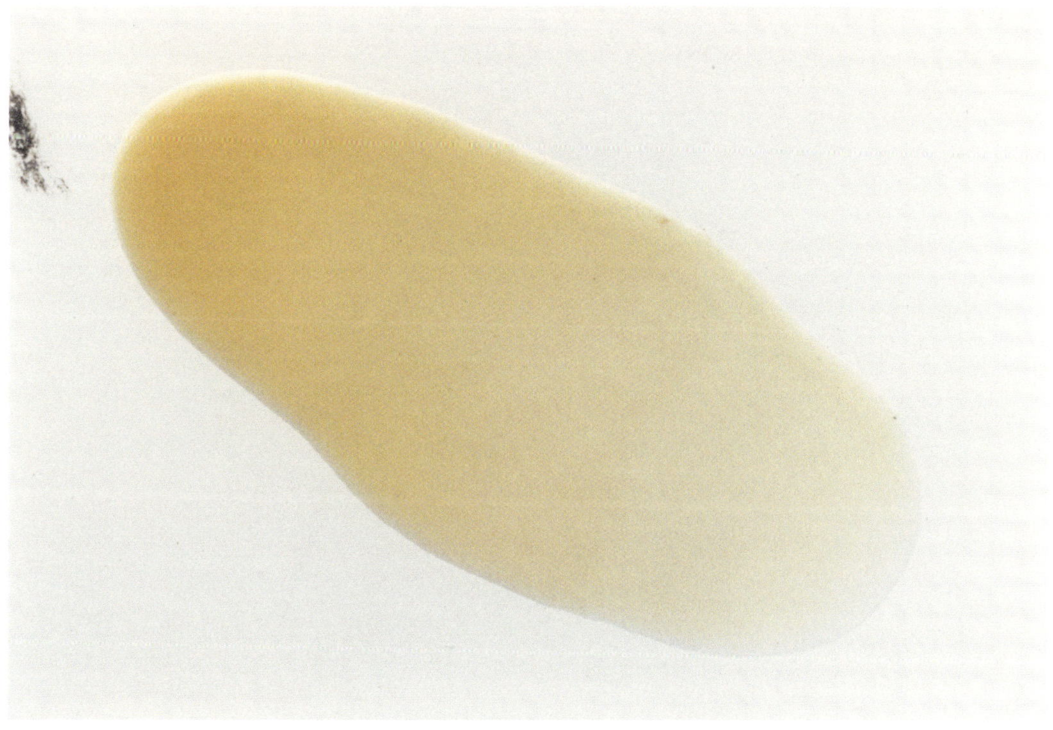

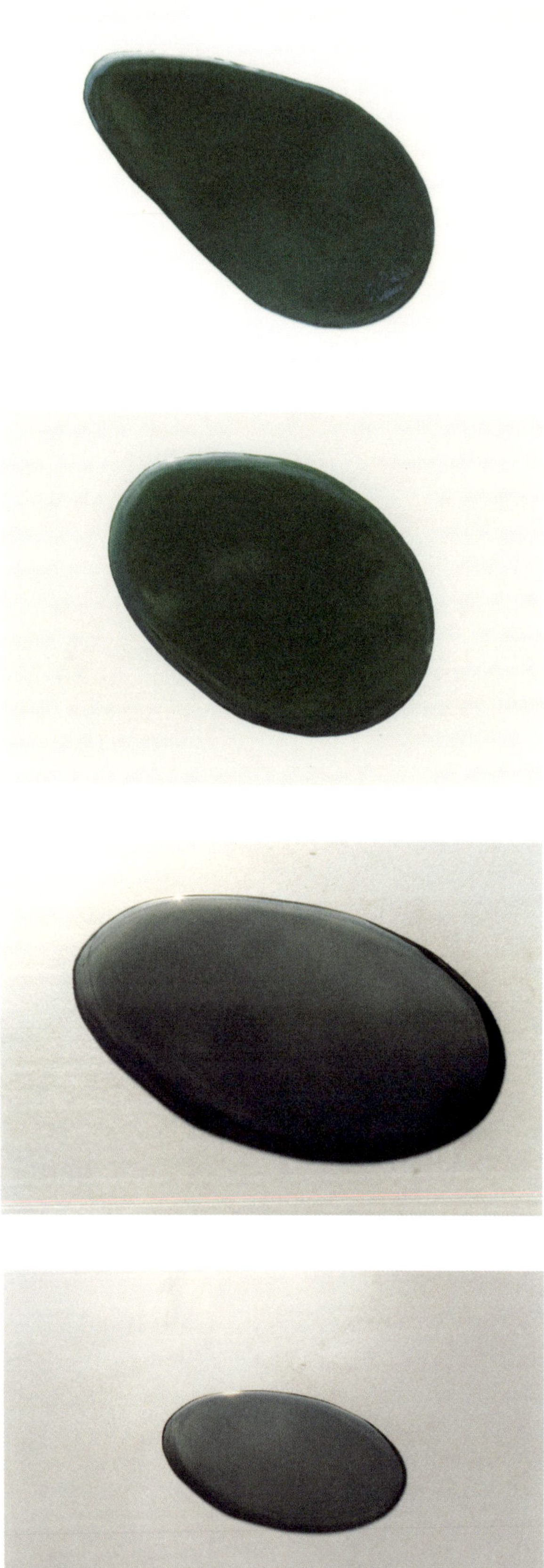

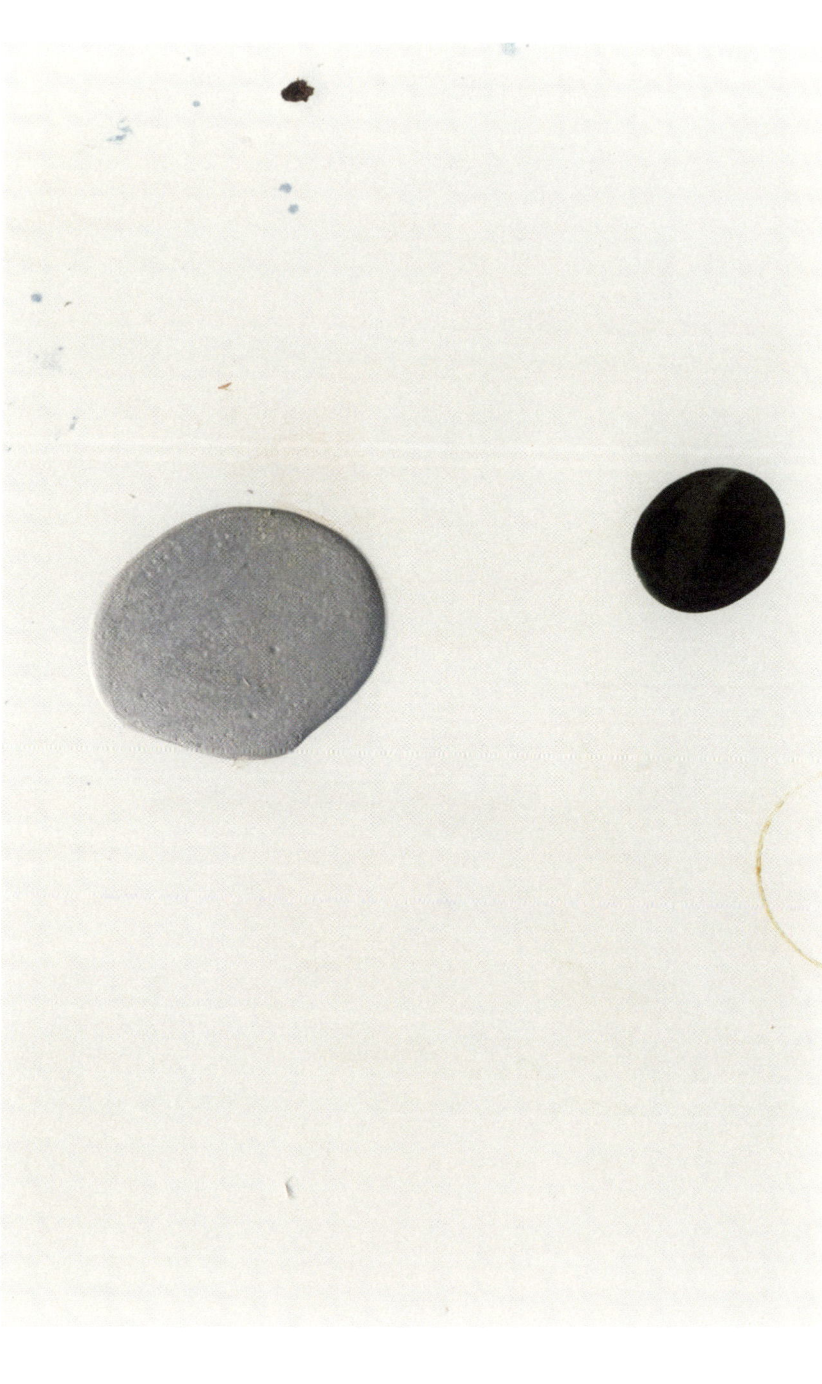

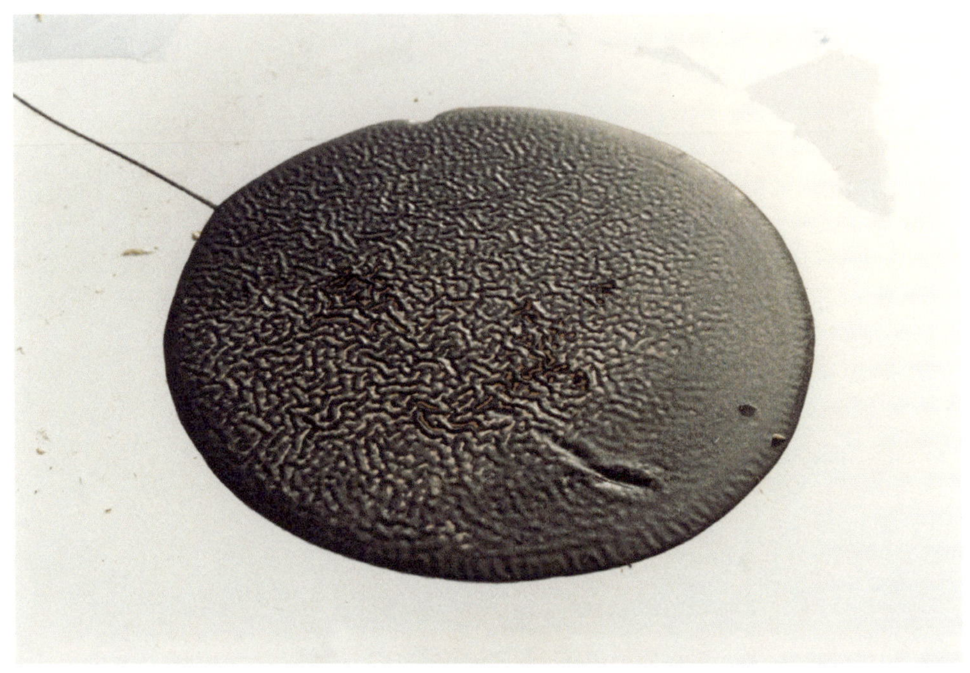

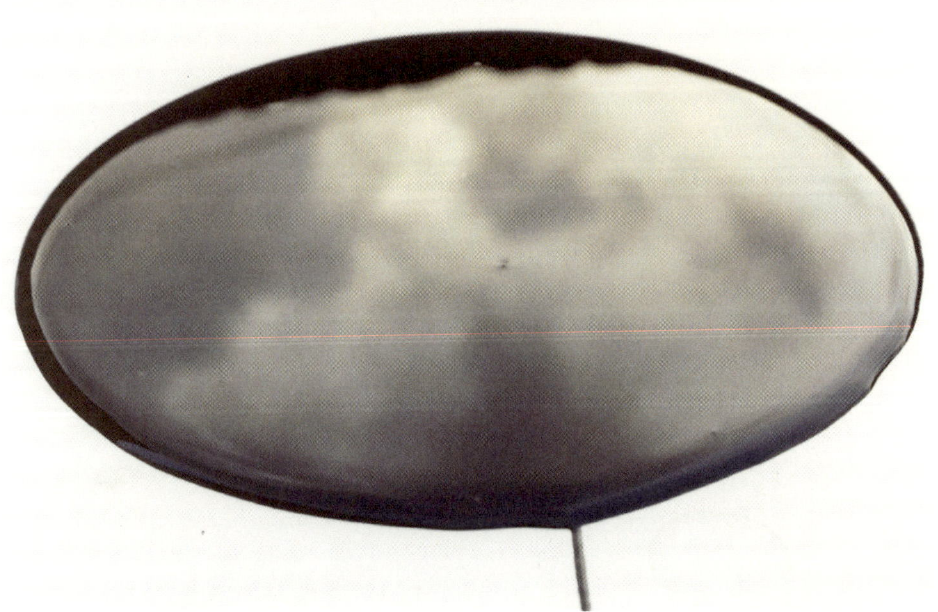

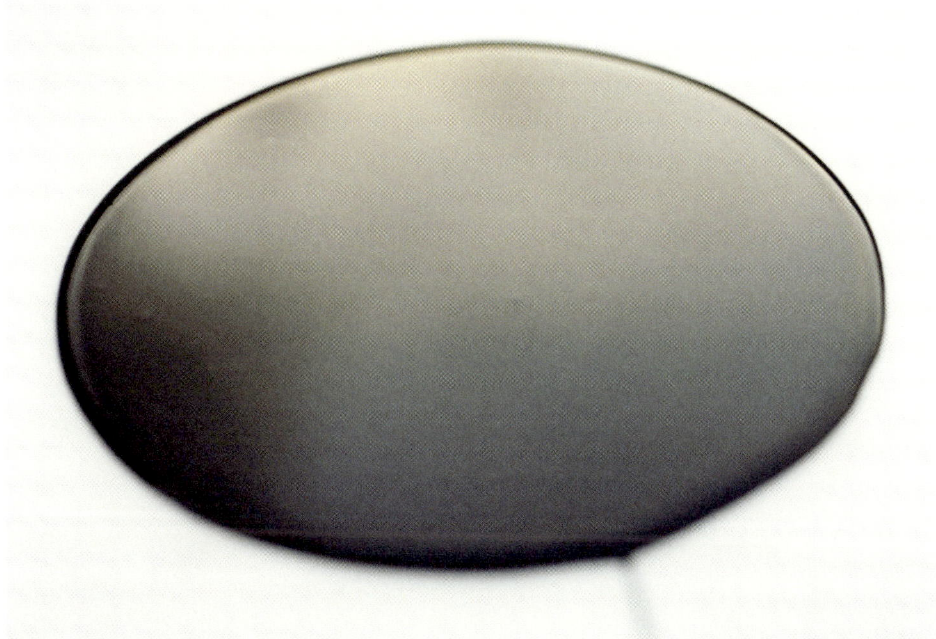

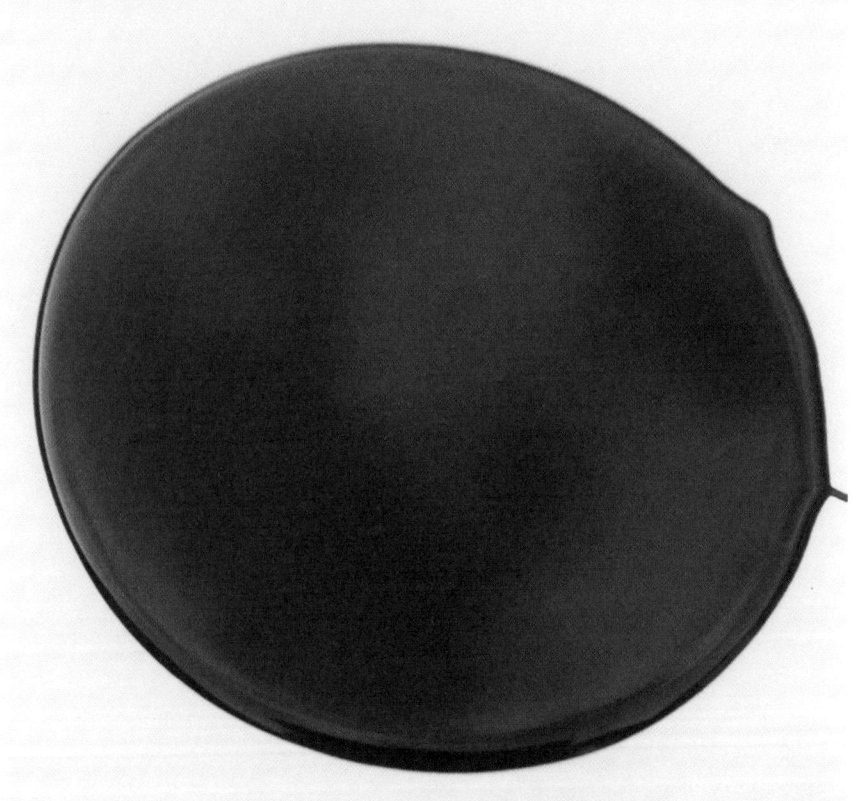

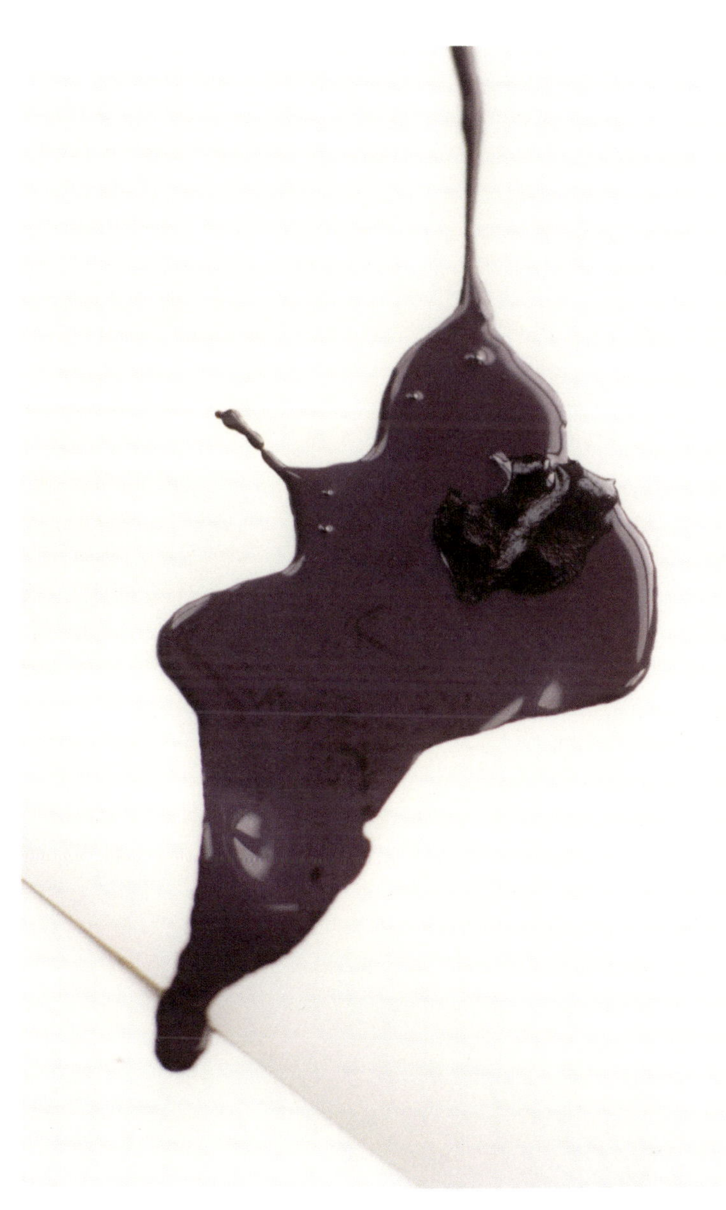

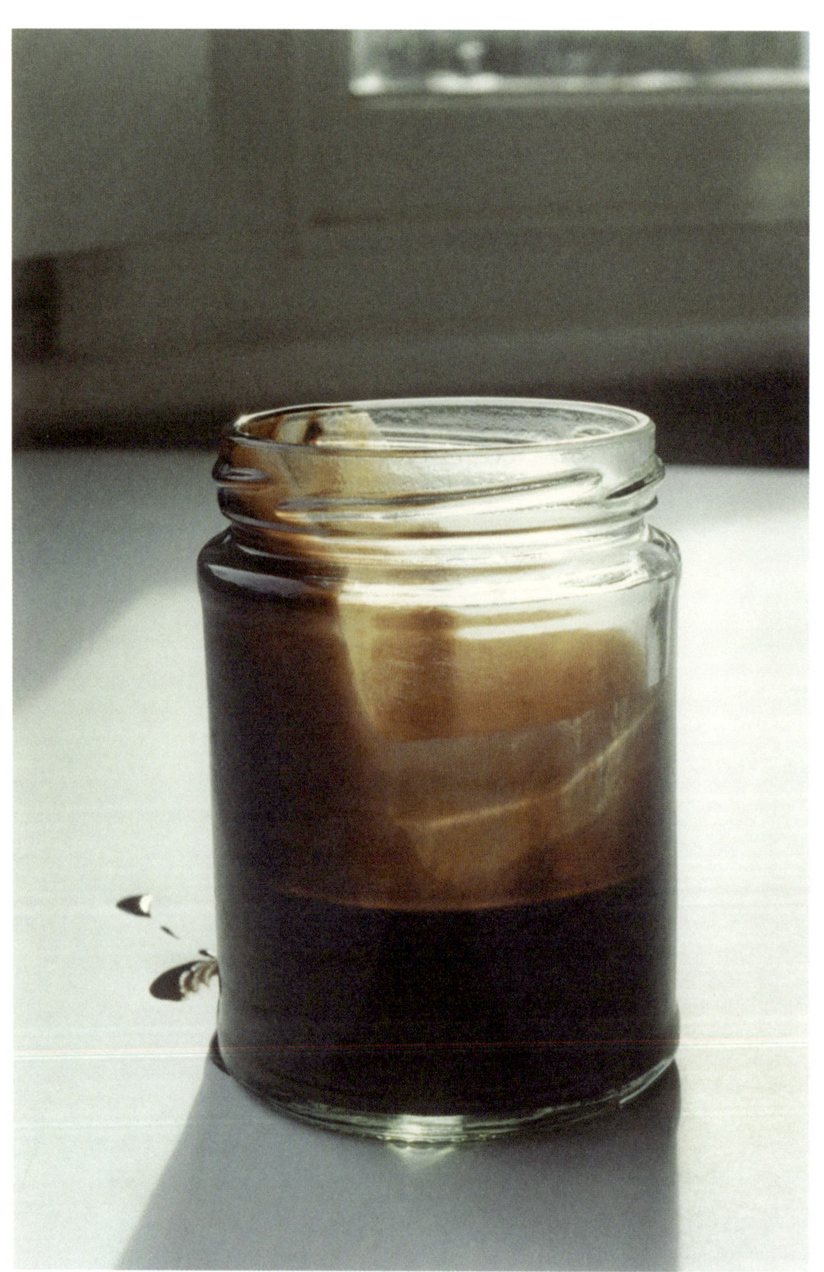

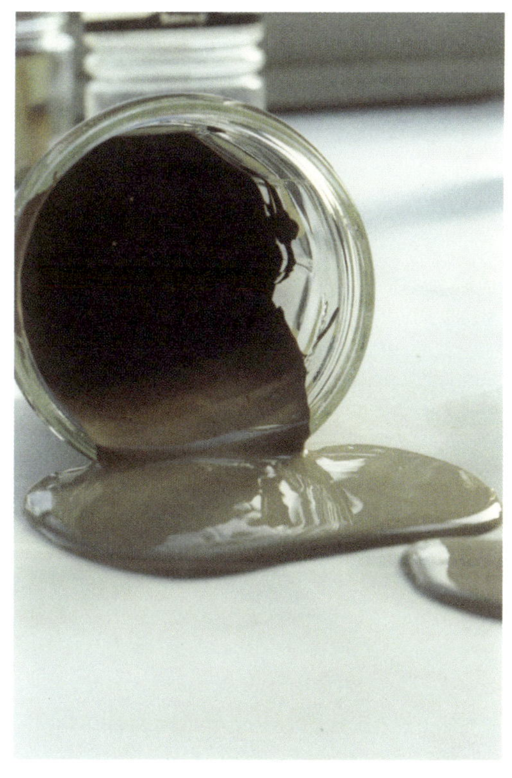

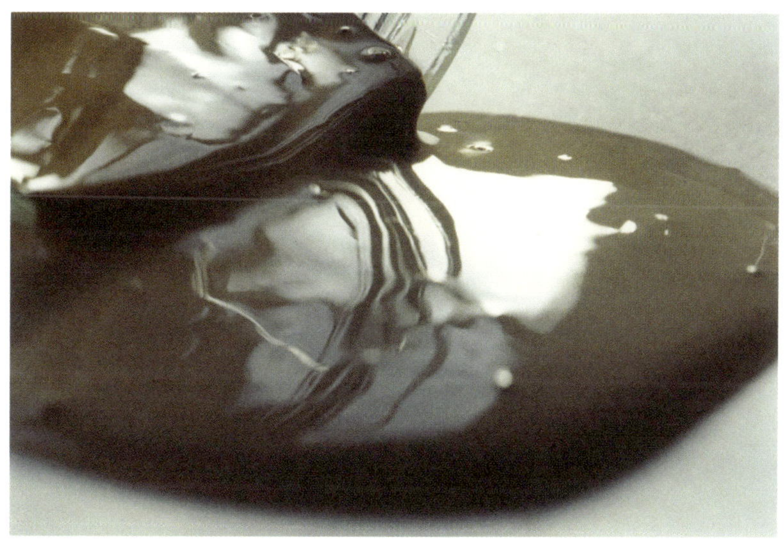

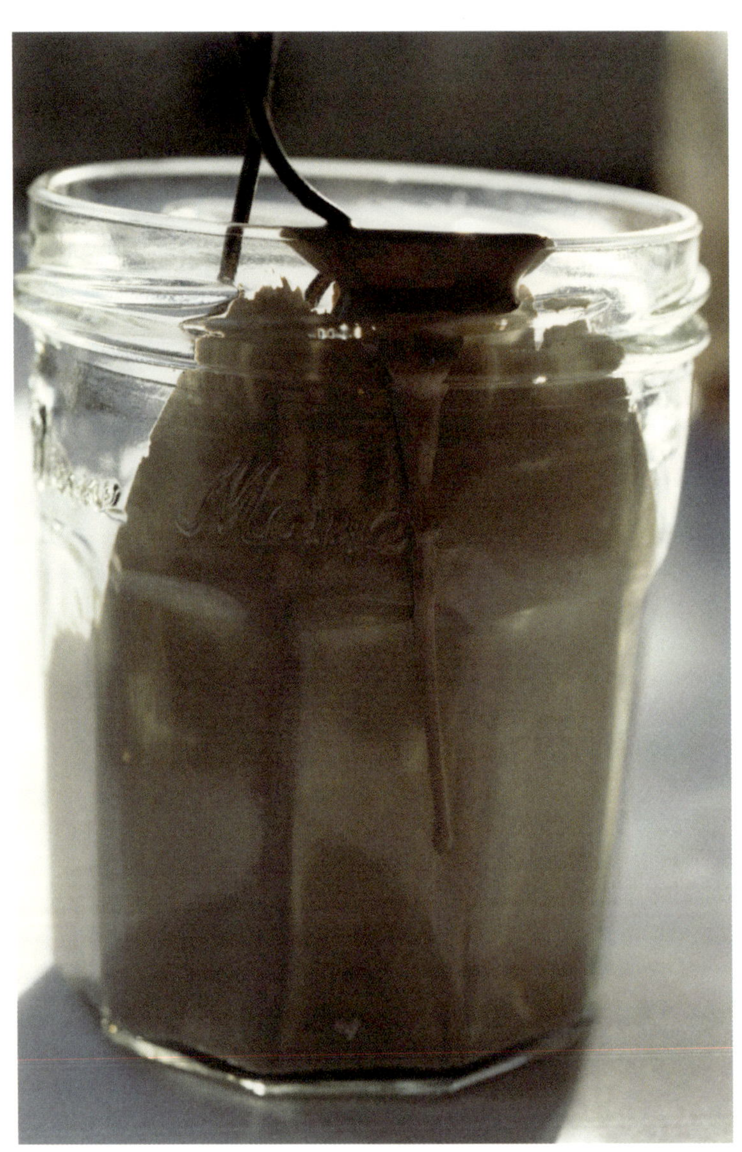

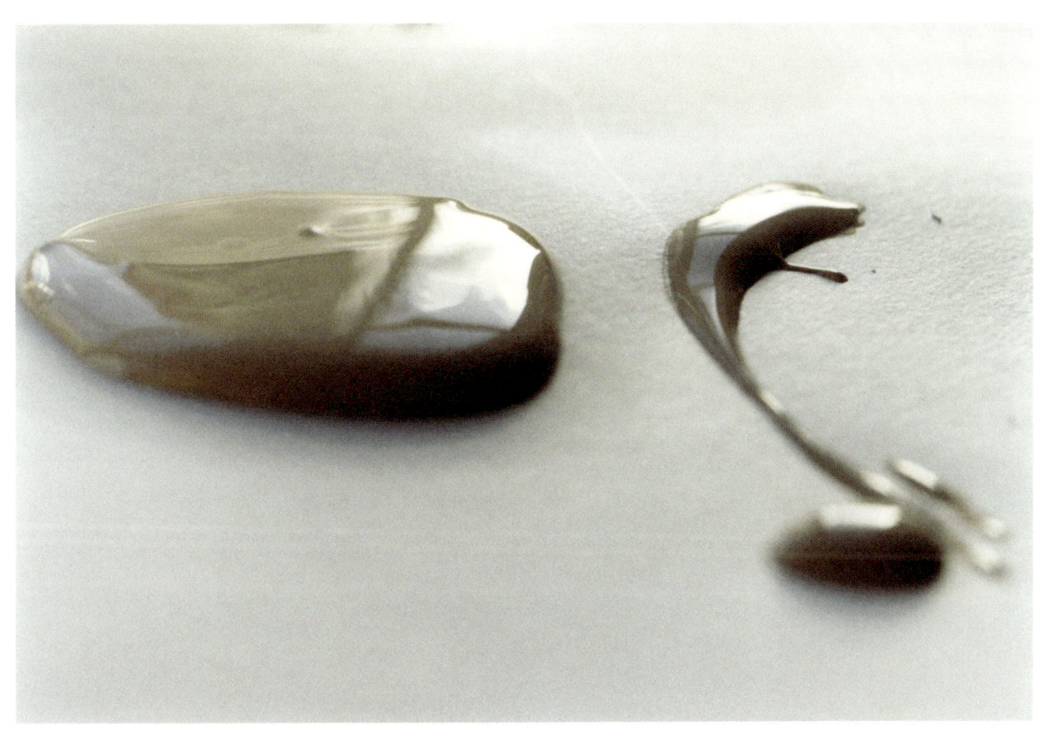

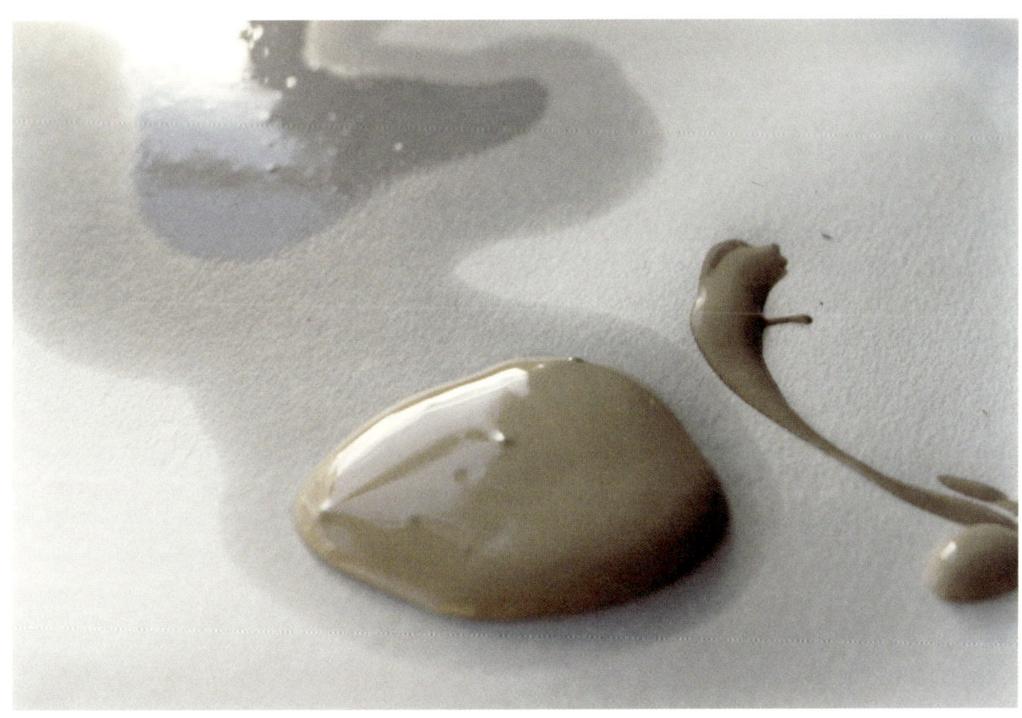

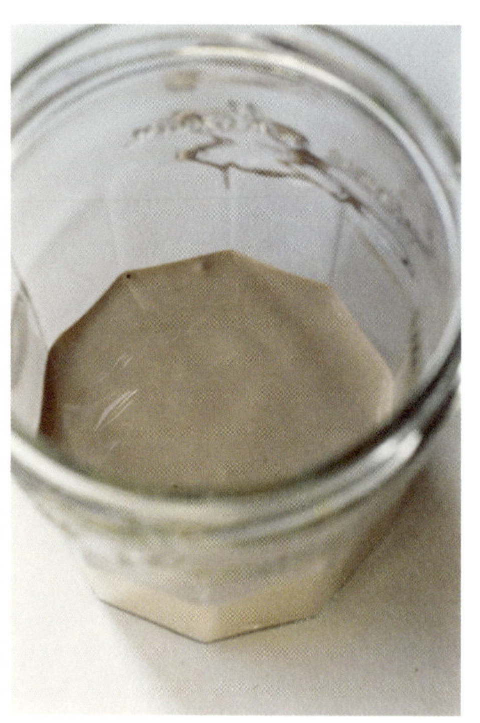

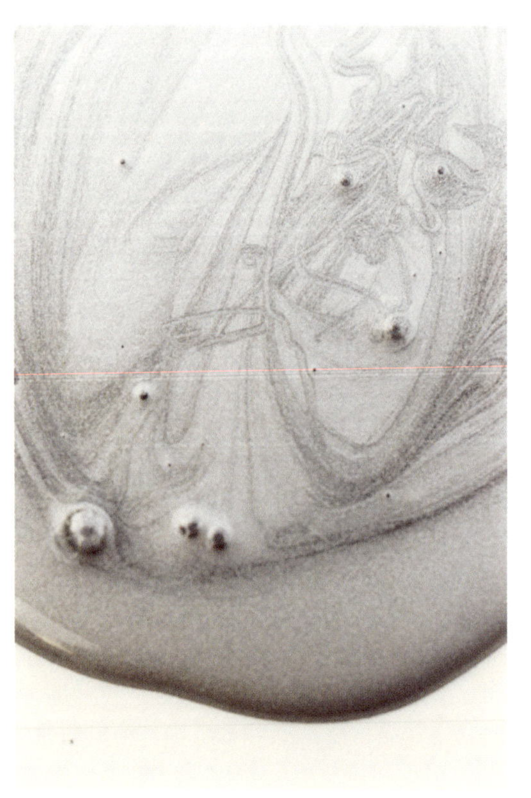

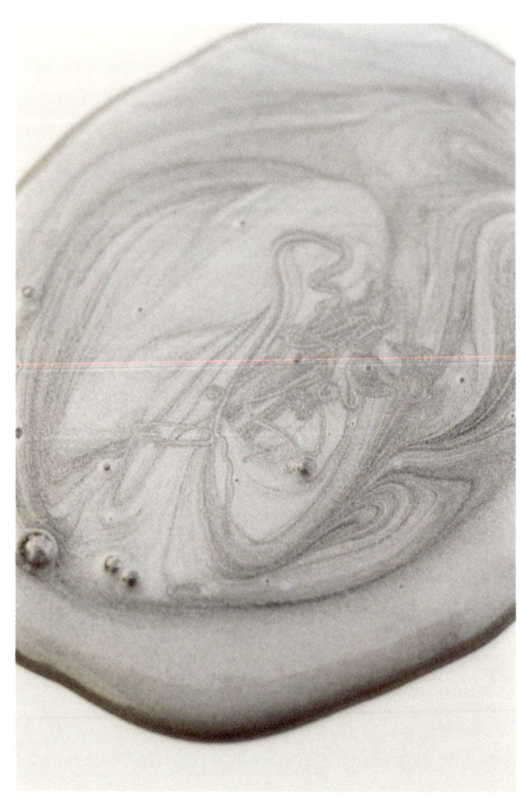

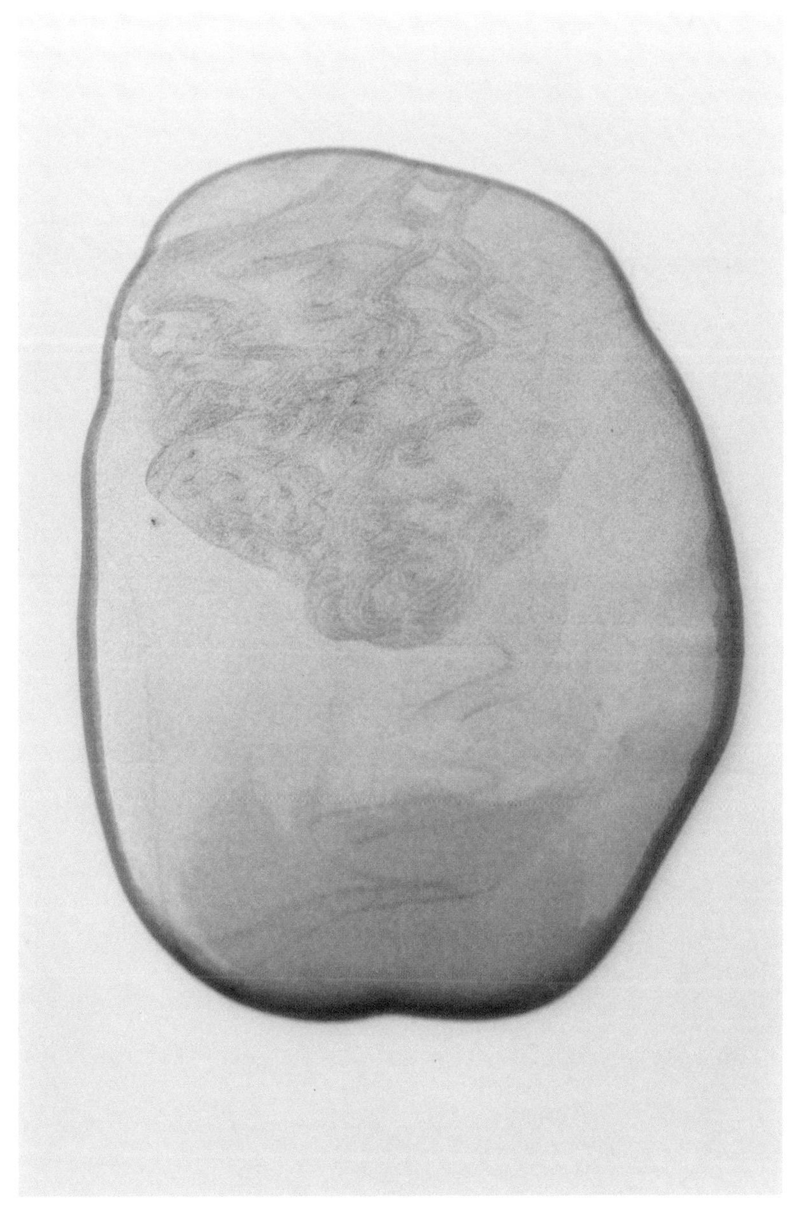

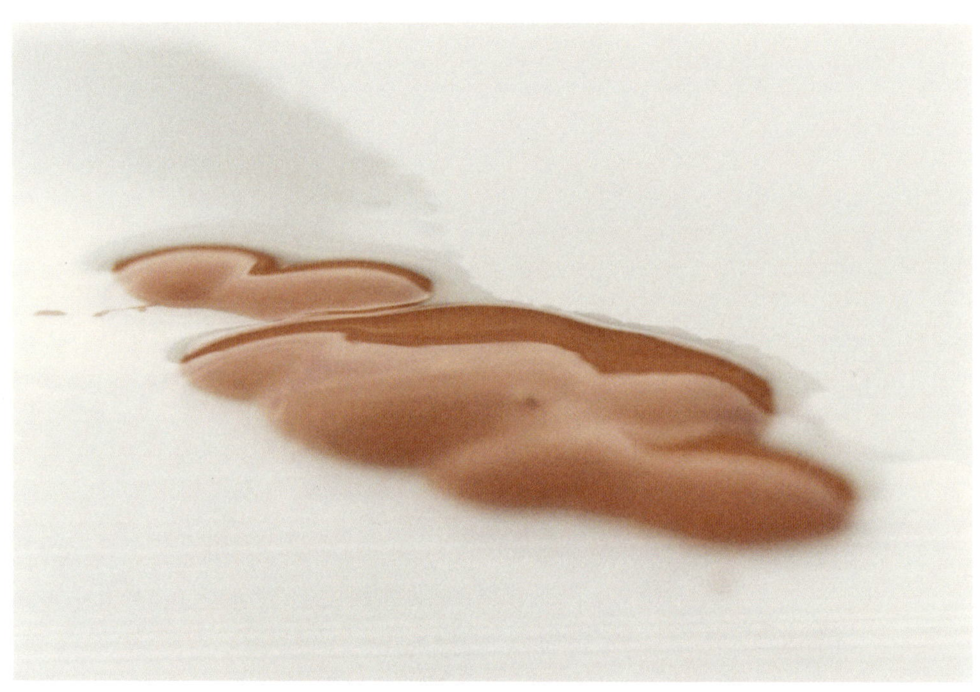

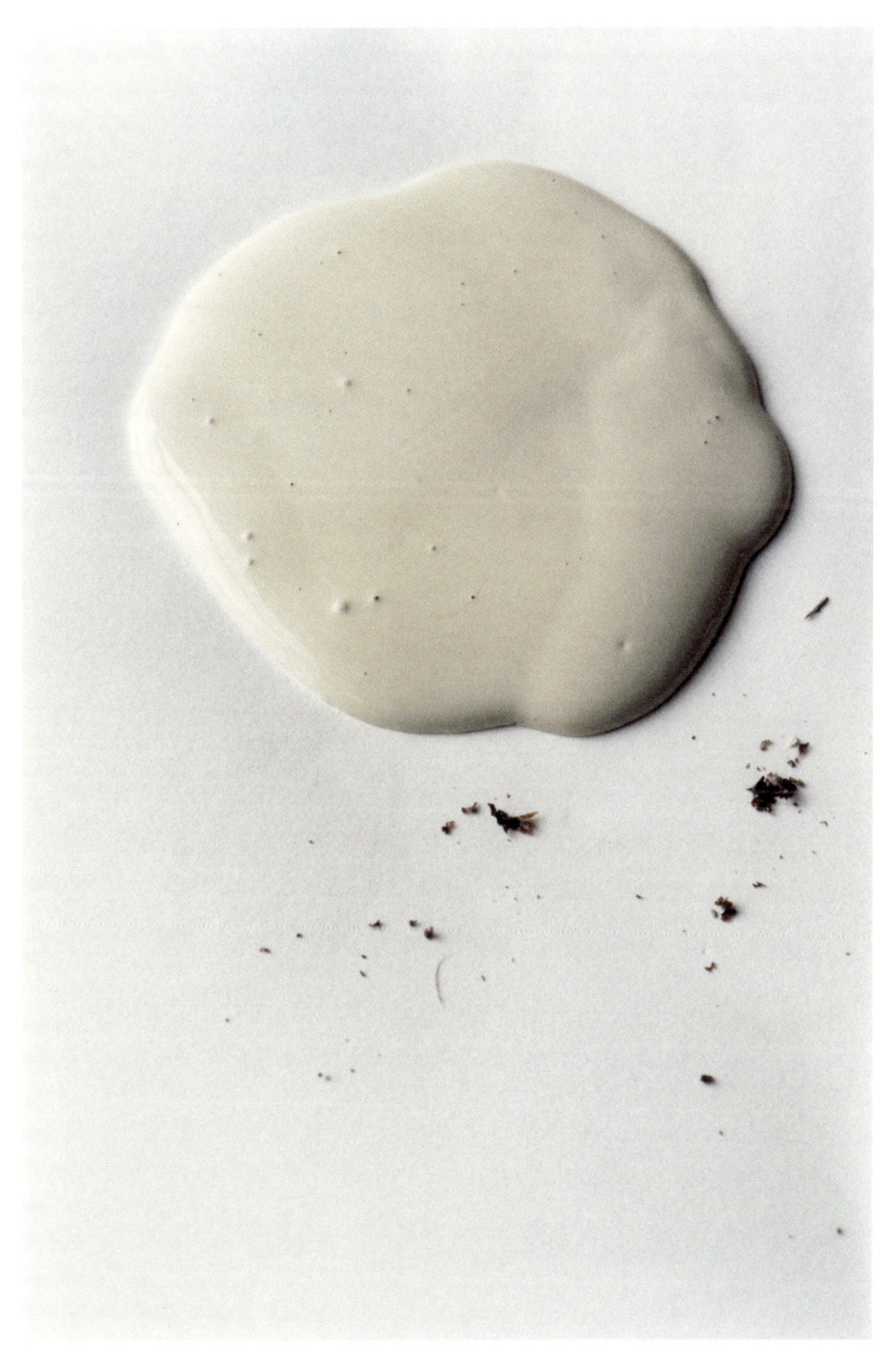

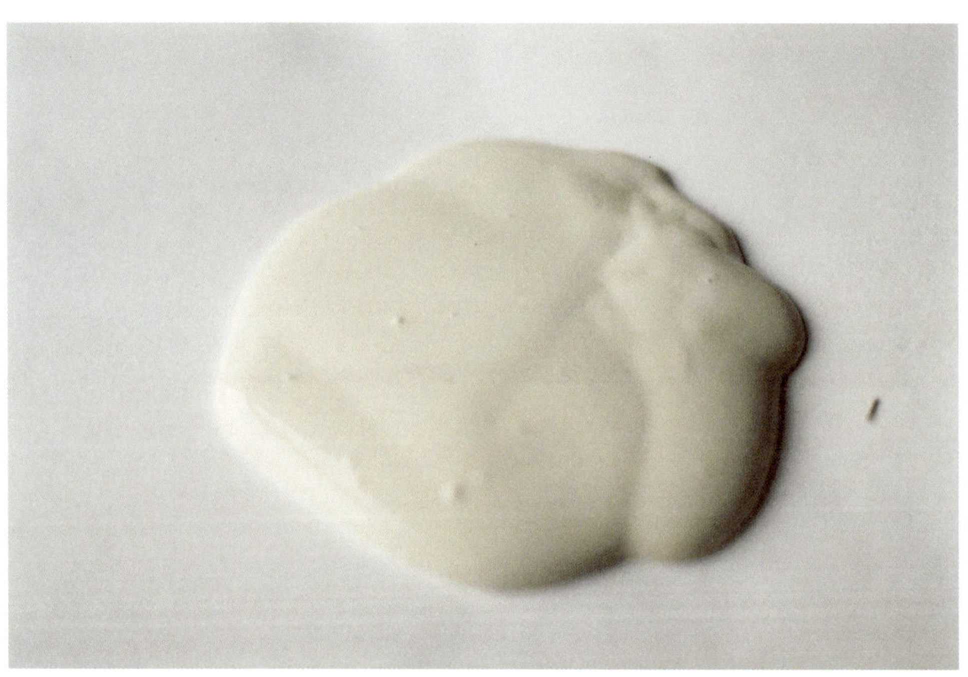

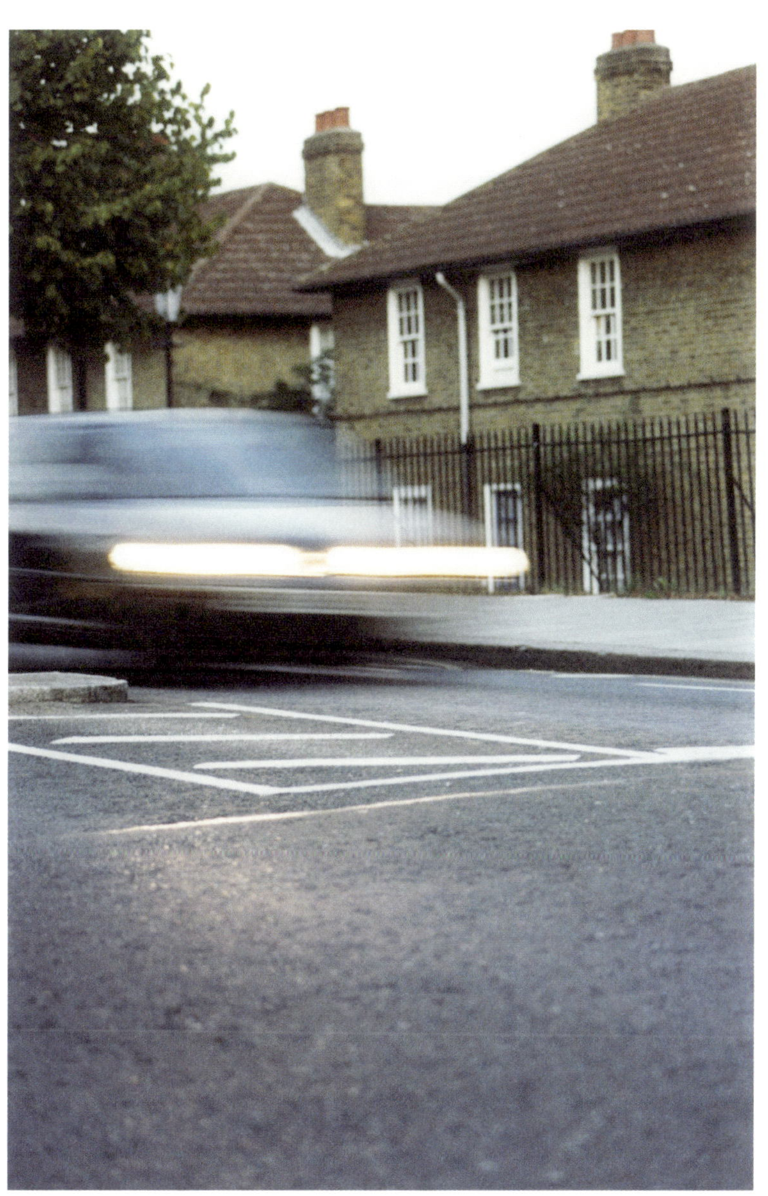

Anders Edström
Safari

First Edition

Thank You Peter Edström, Ulla Edström, Yoshiko Edström and Curtis Winter

Designed by Anders Edström and Lucas Quigley

Published by Nieves
www.nievesbooks.com

ISBN 978-3-905714-58-6

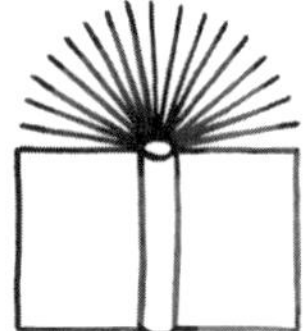

For most people, looking simply happens. There is a view of downtown Los Angeles from my patio, which I daily admire in a disinterested way. I like how my neighbor's terracotta roof foregrounds the silhouettes of skyscrapers miles off and how the dark middle distance slopes towards a façade of pinpoint lights at night. But I have never felt compelled to do anything about it. I sometimes wonder whether if I were a photographer my view would look different, whether my looking would be different. Photography is so various today—especially in art, where internal considerations put a stress on questions of concept and technique—that one may be forgiven the more basic acknowledgment that looking, different kinds of looking, remains its central gist. Some photographers look quickly, letting the world come to them in "decisive moments." Others set the world up, methodically, as if the world's images were already present in their eyes. At least these are the clichés. In reality letting and setting are rarely so opposed.

In Anders Edstrom's *Safari* photographs, for instance, a slow, deliberate looking, a looking focused on a singular subject, a looking that by all appearances holds the outside world at bay, nonetheless reveals an image of openness one might better expect from street or landscape photography, genres bent by time, context, event, and change. But what changes in these *Safari* pictures? Do they have time or context? What is their world?

On the simple level of subject matter, this is not the world Edstrom typically represents, which despite a signature gauziness—as if the air and light he seeks were particulate, thick, or tactile—is one of people and environments interacting. Even more than his tender domestic tableaux or pedestrian portraits, the *Safari* images, made over a two-year period in 2002–2004, are *inside*: the scene, apparently, a studio or a worktable, the range close. So close, in fact, that before one understands that they depict drips or pools of paint on paper, there is an initial sense of abstraction. The soft, existing light pervading the enameled pigments, themselves vibrations of earthy ochres, burnt greens, grays and rusts, suggests a serial display of substance becoming surface—a movement between polish, glaze, and liquid on the one hand and roughness, texture, and mineral on the other. The pleasure, for me, comes in realizing that Edstrom's formal and material reduction is here no different than elsewhere in his work. Subject matter, whatever it is, only serves sensibility.

Describing the latter takes us far from the intimacy of *Safari*, and I will only say that Edstrom is a photographer greatly influenced by his mobility, as the title of this work may suggest. Shaped by his residence in Tokyo no less than his upbringing in Sweden, his work reflects the contingencies of contemporary life (fashion work has been a staple of his photography) as much as a fascination with slow nature. One could write elsewhere about the parallels these photographs may have with the traditional arts of *bonsai* or *ike-bana*, their seeming cultivation of chance-time, or alternately with the European romanticism of their sideways light and setting. But cultural reads should come after the fact rather than justifying it. Is paint is a wild animal to a photographer? Maybe. More likely it is a figure of mental or symbolic space encountered through looking. *Safari interieur.*

—Bennett Simpson